T0154837

THE PANTHER

The Panther

POSTHUMOUS
POEMS

by James Whitehead

Edited by Michael Burns

with an introduction
by James Tabor

Library of Congress Cataloging-in-
Publication Data

Whitehead, James.
  The panther : posthumous poems /
by James Whitehead ; edited by
Michael Burns ; with an introduction
by James Tabor.
     p. cm.
  ISBN 978-0-913785-12-6 (hc.)
  I. Burns, Michael, 1953- II. Title.
PS3573.H48P36 2008
811'.54--dc22
                    2007048138

WE WISH TO THANK DONORS FOR THEIR GENEROSITY
IN UNDERWRITING THE PUBLICATION OF THIS BOOK

"To everything there is a season," says the book of Ecclesiastes, "a time to be born and a time to die." When James Whitehead died unexpectedly in August 2003, none of us could quite believe that such a season could come so soon. He loomed too large in our lives to disappear. As a husband, father, teacher, and friend, he shook the world he walked through, and although we knew he had his quiet moments, it was hard sometimes to imagine him working with his pencil and yellow legal pads in that impossible office of his there on Lafayette Street in Fayetteville, Arkansas. But he did, producing the highly acclaimed novel Joiner early in his career, and going on to publish his distinctive poetry in collections with LSU, Illinois, and U of Missouri Presses. Those poems frame, in artful metrics and dramatic voices, the chief concerns of this man who seemed larger than life, who ultimately made life larger through his voice, the one many can still hear praising or bewailing or offering the many small comforts that we also learned to expect, as much as we did the voice of the tough coach, sailing out over the playing fields of our lives and poems and stories.

Some days we wake to a summer storm and the lines we hear from Ecclesiastes are the ones that claim the right to celebration: "a time to pluck up that which is planted; a time to laugh; a time to dance; a time to speak, and a time for peace."

When I first was blessed to see the unpublished poems that Whitehead had been working on at his death, I knew that they were special. They were courageous; some would say outrageous. But they were also vintage Whitehead. He had often made the dramatic monologue his vehicle for poetry, and the *accentual-syllabic tradition was one he embraced, demonstrating for students and readers the art of good talk and the tension of artifice–the measured line as it shapes the spoken word.*

But we weren't in Mississippi (Jim grew up in Mississippi) or Arkansas anymore. These poems come from the Holy Land, or from the final resting place of their central character, the Roman centurion Tiberius Julius Abdes Pantera. And if, as Ecclesiastes says, there is a time for everything, then somehow the time for these poems came at the wonderful moment that religious scholar Dr. James Tabor was himself writing about the origins of the historical Jesus. His book, The Jesus Dynasty, *is not one Whitehead could have read or known about, and the connection between the quests of these two people seems even more wondrous because of that.*

My work as editor of these poems was made easier by the fact that Whitehead had arranged and named them, and most of them were complete and needed little editing. I would like to thank friends and colleagues, especially Miller Williams, for their help as I made careful decisions about which poems to include in this collection. And my special thanks goes to Gen Whitehead-Broyles, who trusted me to take the poems and share them, as they should have been shared, with the world. I remember asking Miller, one of Jim's lifelong friends, what he thought Jim would like to see come of these poems. And his answer was, "Well, I think he'd love to see them in a book you could put on a chain and hang around your neck." With the fine help of Dr. Tabor's introduction, I believe we have that book. So we send it out to Whitehead's readers, old and new. It is a time to heal and laugh and dance.

Michael Dean Burns

TABLE OF CONTENTS

TABLE OF CONTENTS

Twin Quests Intersecting out of Time

Everyone even remotely connected to Christian culture knows the basic outlines of the Christmas Story. Mary, a virgin, is engaged to marry Joseph in the little town of Nazareth in Galilee. She has a vision in which the angel Gabriel tells her she will become pregnant through the Holy Spirit, and that her child will be the Son of God and Messiah, having no human father. This story, passed on in two versions in Matthew and Luke, dates back to the late decades of the first century AD, nearly a hundred years after Jesus' birth. Our earliest gospel, Mark, relates no birth story at all and, in fact, calls Jesus the "son of

Mary" (Mark 6:3) without naming a father, which in Jewish culture implies something irregular. It seems that Jesus grew up with rumors that his birth involved some kind of scandal. His enemies taunt him at one point, "We were not born of fornication" (John 8:41). It is interesting that Christians who take the virgin birth story literally, and historians who take the illegitimacy tradition seriously, find strange agreement—Joseph married Mary, but he was not the father of Jesus. So who was?

Strangely, there is a name that is passed down in sources outside the New Testament. Jesus is called the "son of Pantera," a Greek name meaning *Panther*. But who might this Panther have been and what is behind the legend?

Not too long after the publication of my book, *The Jesus Dynasty* (2006), which includes an historical analysis of the Panther evidence, I heard from a friend that a poet at the University of Arkansas had done extensive research on the Panther and had written some marvelous poems that explored imaginatively the relationship between the young Mary and her lover, Pantera. The friend did not have the poet's name (who had recently died), and I put the information in the back of my mind, intending at some point to pursue it further. Shortly thereafter, Michael Burns, an English professor at Missouri State University, contacted me. A former student of James Whitehead, the deceased poet, Burns had been given these poems by Whitehead's widow, Gen Whitehead-Broyles, and hoped to publish them. It turns out that he heard of a lecture I gave on Pantera, so he sent me a few samples. I have to say, I was utterly "blown away" by the craft and power of Whitehead's vision.

11

James Whitehead had become fascinated with the Pantera legend when he first read about it in Morton Smith's *Jesus the Magician* (1978); in this book, the late, great historian describes a tombstone in Germany, one belonging to a Roman soldier named Pantera. Smith made the passing suggestion that this tombstone might be our only "genuine relic of the Holy Family."Whitehead's poetic soul was fired by the idea that the young Mary might have loved and become pregnant by this young man from Palestine who ended up a Roman soldier, dying at age 62 on the German frontier. He plunged himself into research on every bit of evidence he could uncover on Pantera and on what it might have been like to be a Roman soldier serving in Palestine and then in Germany in the first century AD. Beginning in the summer of 2001, Whitehead made trips to Germany to visit the tombstone; he was accompanied by two young German archaeologists, Peter Haupt and Sabine Hornung, who guided him in his research and became attached to him and his Quest.

As it turns out, Whitehead was not the first poet to be inspired by an historian's investigation of this tombstone. In 1909, Thomas Hardy wrote a long and passionate poem entitled "Pantera," having heard about the legend through Adolf Deissmann's German article, "Der Name Panthera" (1906). Hardy's poem recounts the romantic and sexual love between a teenaged Mary and a Roman soldier named Panthera, stationed in Palestine. Hardy portrays the aging Panthera, who thinks back on his life and on what he has left behind. The poem can surely be read against the backdrop of the poet's general aversion to conventional forms of religious authority and Christian tradition. However, I think that Hardy, like Whitehead, found in the Pantera story an apt expression of the most touching aspects of our universal humanness: of love, of separation, of the uncharted life of a child, and of all they might mean to one old and thinking back on it all. And who could better portray the "human, all-too-human" than the enshrined Mary, mother of God, and her divine Son, Jesus Christ of Nazareth? It is not just that Hardy disbelieved such orthodoxies; he also wanted these figures, the chief symbols of all that is heavenly and perfect and removed from our world, to end up serving that very thing—our very human existence on this planet, so filled with hope yet fraught with uncertainties, foolishness, and finally death. I have to wonder if James Whitehead might have been influenced by Hardy's work, though he surely forges his own imaginative account of things.

But back to the history. What do we really know about Pantera? And what about the tombstone in Germany?

The earliest version of the Pantera story comes from a Greek philosopher named Celsus. In an anti-Christian work titled *On the True Doctrine,* written around 178 AD, Celsus relates a tale that Mary "was pregnant by a Roman soldier named Panthera," and was driven away by her husband as an adulterer. It is unlikely that Celsus invented this name or the occupation of the man that he insists was the biological father of Jesus. He is repeating what he has heard circulating in Jewish circles. The name itself appears even earlier. The well-known rabbi Eliezer ben Hyrcanus, who lived around the end of the 1st century AD, relates a teaching told to him by Jacob of Sikhnin, a Galilean follower of Jesus who lived in the town of Sepphoris. Some have identified this Jacob as the grandson of Jesus' youngest brother, Jude. Jacob passes on the teaching "in the name of Jesus the son of Panteri." There is also a dispute among these early rabbis (involving this same Jacob, follower of Jesus) as to whether or not it is permissible to heal a snakebite in the "name of Jesus son of Panter." These early sources say nothing of why Jesus would be called "son of Pantera," nor do they identify Pantera as a Roman soldier; what they do show is that Jesus is identified by this name quite early in Galilee and that the name could be used without explanation or qualification. Some later Christian scholars held that Pantera was a term of abusive slang, a play on the Greek word *parthenos,* which means "virgin." But the two words don't match and there is no evidence of Jesus being commonly called "son of a virgin" in Galilee this early (which would otherwise provide fuel for the pun). Others have suggested that Jesus was slanderously called "son of a Panther" in reference to the wild and lustful nature of his real father. The problem with these suggestions is that the earliest references to Jesus as "son of Pantera" are not derisive or polemical. In Judaism, when you want to identify a person you attach the name of the father. That is the clear sense of these earliest references: they are intended to identify, not to malign.

Of one thing we can be sure: Pantera is a real name, not a concocted term of slander. In his 1906 article, Adolf Deissmann detailed the various ancient inscriptions that used the name Pantera/Panthera in and around the first century AD. He showed conclusively that the name was in use during that time and was especially favored by Roman soldiers. One particular example that he cited stood out. It was an inscribed tombstone of one Tiberius Julius Abdes Pantera, discovered in a Roman cemetery in 1859 at Bingerbrück (just twelve miles north of Bad Kreuznach, where the Nahe River meets the Rhine). Deissmann included a photo showing the carved figure of a Roman soldier with the neck and head broken off and a clearly preserved Latin inscription under his feet that reads:

TIBERIUS JULIUS ABDES PANTERA

OF SIDON, AGED 62

A SOLDIER OF 40 YEARS SERVICE,

OF THE 1ST COHORT OF ARCHERS,

LIES HERE

Deissmann noted that this particular "Pantera" had come to Germany from Palestine and had died in the middle of the first century AD. This and nine other gravestones of Roman soldiers had been uncovered quite by accident in October, 1859, during the construction of the railway station at Bingerbrück. They had been collected first by the local historical society, then put on display in 1933 in the old city museum, and are now in the newly constructed Römerhalle in the little town of Bad Kreuznach. In October, 2005, as part of my research for *The Jesus Dynasty,* I traveled to Germany to examine these artifacts firsthand.

Pantera's full name is given formally in the inscription as: Tiberius Julius Abdes Pantera. Pantera was his surname. The

15

names Tiberius Julius are cognomens or acquired names. They indicate that Pantera was not a native born Roman but a former slave who became a freedman and, for his service in the army, received the rights of Roman citizenship from Tiberius Caesar. Initial enlistments were for twenty-five years but Pantera made a career out of the military, serving for forty years until his death at age sixty-two. Since the emperor Tiberius came to rule in 14 AD, we can assume that Pantera's death was some years after this date and was likely from natural causes, since he had enlisted in the army when he was just 22. The name Abdes is Pantera's praenomen or given name. It is most interesting. It is a Latinized version of an Aramaic name ('ebed) meaning "servant of God," indicating that Pantera was of Semitic or even Jewish background, whether native born, a convert, or from a family sympathetic to Judaism. He may have been Jewish. The name Pantera is Greek, even though it appears here in a Latin inscription. In 1891, the French archaeologist Clermont-Ganneau made a surprising discovery. In a first century Jewish tomb on the Nablus road (just north of the Old City of Jerusalem), there was an ossuary with the name Pentheros in Greek, as well as the name Josepos or Joseph, the son of this Pentheros. We know from the burials that they were Jewish, which gives us definitive evidence that the name Pentheros/Pantera was used in the time of Jesus by Jews as well as Romans.

Abdes Pantera was from Sidon, a coastal town of Syria-Palestine, just north of Tyre, which is less than 40 miles from Sepphoris, the town of which Nazareth is a suburb. We know that this particular cohort of archers had come to Dalmatia (Croatia) in the year 6 AD from Palestine and was moved to the Rhine/ Nahe river area in 9 AD. It should not surprise us that Pantera died and was buried in Germany, as were so many thousands of other Roman soldiers who fought in the terrible frontier wars around the time of Jesus. Augustus even transferred Varus, the legate of Syria, to command the Roman legions just north of this very area of Germany. The Romans retained permanent outposts in Germany, and the Bingerbrück cemetery provides us with evidence that veterans lived out their lives on the frontier. Based on the coin evidence found at the cemetery, the style of the gravestones, and the content of their inscriptions, the other nine tombstones appear to date from around the same period: mid- to late- first century AD.

Is it remotely plausible that, among all the thousands of tomb inscriptions of the period, this might be the tombstone of Jesus' father—and in Germany of all places? The chances seem infinitesimal, but the evidence should not be dismissed out of hand. Pantera was a Roman soldier, possibly a Jew; he was a native of Syria-Palestine, just north of Galilee; and he was a contemporary of Mary, mother of Jesus. So we have the right name, the right occupation, the right place, and the right time.

It is also important to resist the assumption that being the son of a Roman soldier necessarily implied something negative. John the Baptizer was quite accommodating to Roman soldiers who came out to hear him preach, and the earliest description we have indicates that John even baptized Roman soldiers, who then became part of the Messianic movement sparked by John and his kinsman, Jesus (Luke 3:14). Several Roman officers were praised for their spirituality and piety in the New Testament, and some were part of Jesus' earliest following. In fact, Jesus commended a Roman centurion at Capernaum, a city on the Sea of Galilee, as having more faith than anyone he had encountered–including his fellow Jews (Luke 7:9). It was also a Roman centurion who declared of Jesus at his death, "Surely this was a son of God" (Mark 15:39).

Some who give historical weight to the "Jesus son of Pantera" tradition have suggested that a Roman soldier may have raped Mary. Given the times and turbulent circumstances surrounding Jesus' birth, such a possibility exists. As jolting as such an idea initially sounds, some have found in this scenario a compelling expression of acceptance and unconditional love, certainly by Mary as the mother, but also by Joseph as the husband, who was willing to adopt the child as his own. An alternative would be that Mary became pregnant through a relationship she had chosen. Since we know nothing of the possible circumstances surrounding Mary's pregnancy and her relationship to Jesus' father (Roman soldier or not), there is no reason to postulate something ugly or sinister. We do not know any details of the circumstances surrounding Mary's betrothal to Joseph. Was she a willing participant in an arranged marriage to an older man? Had she formed a prior relationship with another man? Our Pantera buried in Germany would have been a younger man closer to Mary's age at the time of the birth of Jesus. My point is that we simply do not know–so we should not pass judgment and make negative assumptions as soon as the phrase, "Roman soldier" is put before us. Jesus' enemies would have made the worst of things and freely used the labels "fornication" and "whore." There is no reason to endorse their assumptions. When it comes to family scandal, unwed pregnancies, and broken engagements, the street gossip of a rural Galilean village is the last place one wants to turn for any objectivity.

There is one other piece of this puzzle that may be significant. It is one of the most curious stories in Mark, our earliest gospel. Remember, Mark is the one who called Jesus "the son of Mary" and never mentions Joseph or Jesus' birth at all. Mark abruptly reports a mysterious side-trip taken by Jesus when he is operating around the Sea of Galilee:

> And from there he arose, and went away into the borders of Tyre and Sidon. And he entered into a house, and would have no man know it; and he could not be hid (Mark 7:24)

We are also told that, as he returned, he went through Sidon back to the Sea of Galilee, not the most direct route (Mark 7:31). No one has ever really explained his reason for doing so. Luke has no idea what to do with this story, so he simply drops it. Matthew includes it, but he carefully deletes the part about Jesus entering a specific house where he is known, and he removes the details regarding the return route through Sidon (Matt 15:21, 29). Perhaps the information was irrelevant to him, or perhaps he wanted to avoid having his readers raise the obvious question: why would Jesus abruptly leave the territory of Herod Antipas in Galilee and travel to Syria to the coastal areas of Tyre and Sidon? And whose house is this that he knows and secretly enters? Remember, these are not Jewish cities. It is also noteworthy that Jesus regularly praises the cities of Tyre and Sidon as being potentially more open to his message than the cities of the Galilee, where he mostly preached (Luke 10:14). Tyre and Sidon are not remote areas from Galilee, and we are told that crowds of people from both Tyre and Sidon came to the northern side of the Sea of Galilee to hear Jesus preach (Luke 6:17). Just as there is a positive treatment of Roman soldiers in the gospels, there is a remarkably favorable view of these two Gentile coastal cities. Is it possible or even likely that there is a connection? It seems that the abrupt nature of the story, strangely passed on by Mark, hints at something more.

I am convinced—and our best evidence indicates—that Joseph, who married the pregnant Mary, was not the father of Jesus. Jesus' father remains unknown, but he was possibly named Pantera; and he quite possibly was (or subsequently became) a Roman soldier. The gravestone in Germany, whether that of Jesus' father or not, serves as a tangible reminder of the possibility of a love between Mary and Jesus' father that has been wholly eliminated from Christian theology.

I am deeply moved that my own historical Quest and the poetic Quest of James Whitehead were so closely intertwined, even though they never intersected in time. Somehow (and without knowing it) we found each other, standing in front of a 1900-year-old tombstone in Germany, both touched by the imagination of human love and the reality of life's complex contours. Whitehead's poems are a testimony to that bond and

I hope that, through this beautiful book, the vision we shared can spread further. For, as Whitehead's Gabriel puts it to Panthera, "Your son in Galilee is magical!" Surely he remains so to this day.

James D. Tabor
June, 2007, Jerusalem

The Panther

A CONFUSION BEGINS
AT THE FIRST GARDEN CEMETERY
OF THE SOMME I VISIT

In late May, the green fields of Picardy
Are beautiful. Perfection comes to mind,
And all the roads so carefully maintained
It seems I'll never say *catastrophe*
And grief-stricken fall down to one knee,
Weeping for soldiers, those we read are buried
Where they fell, or near, in no man's land.
These roads and fields deny futility

As does the garden cemetery here.
Each rank of white Portland headstones
Features pink roses, and flowers I don't know.
Many stones say, *A Soldier of the Great War,*
While others give the regiments and names
Of those who died here, and, finally, below
A date of death, a show
Of sentiment—*He was our loving son . . . .*

Or—Jesus! — *Dulce et Decorum est* . . . .
A troubling, orderly scene,
Wheatfields and garden saying bless, bless,
And then one stone: *Lord, help us bear our loss.*

AFTER A BRIEF POSTING TO JERUSALEM, TIBERIUS JULIUS ABDES PANTERA, A SIDONIAN ARCHER, WALKS TOWARD EVENING BEYOND THE CITY WALLS

*—It is possible, though not likely, that his tombstone
from Bingerbrück is our only genuine relic of the Holy Family?*

—Morton Smith

Another crucifixion, another prophet
Hanged between two thugs, and women crying,
The women of the prophet more than likely,
The eldest one his mother,
Wearing a blue shawl, a mighty sorrow—
And the Panther, old soldier, is moved by her.
Something about her mouth—her fingers fluttering
Beyond her narrow wrists—her arms outstretched.
Something wants to be remembered clearly.

But what's for memory this afternoon
In a place of skulls, a memory of girls
In Galilee or Rome, Transalpine Gaul
Or Spain? —The prophet is calling to his God,

A sorry end, and the Panther goes away
Remembering a bow he fashioned once
As a boy in Sidon fifty years ago,
His destiny of arrows.

I am an archer,
The first cohort for almost forty years
My family! He reminds himself
He'll dream of her open mouth,
Wake to orders, return to Bingerbrück.

IN JERUSALEM BARRACKS
TIBERIUS JULIUS ABDES PANTERA
DREAMS OF MIRIAM THE HAIRDRESSER
THE NIGHT BEFORE HE BEGINS
HIS JOURNEY HOME TO BINGERBRÜCK

Of course the Panther didn't know of Dürer's pictures
Or the medieval forgery
That says the Christ had lovely hair
The color of unripe hazel and smooth to the ears,

But from the ears down slightly darker-colored corkscrew curls,
More glistening, and waving downward from the shoulders,
Pilate's description of the Nazarene.

Caught in a crown of thorns the dead man's hair
Was pitiful, distressed, except for curls
That fell corkscrewing down so prettily,
All this somehow more terrible than the nails.

The old archer's grey hair was still curly
And he probably looked a lot like Albrecht Dürer
Toward the end, vain and circumspect,
Until near dawn he came into a dream,

His final dream of women,
Especially a Galilean girl
Named Miriam, who once did oil his hair.

THE FATHER OF JESUS IS DYING

Tiberius Julius Abdes Pantera
of Sidon, aged 62,
a soldier of 40 years' service,
of the first cohort of archers
lies here

—tombstone near Bingerbrück

They've fixed him spelt and kidney beans
With sage leaves and virgin olive oil, of course,
To say nothing of onions and sausages,
Garlic, venison, and marjoram.
He's feted so well he knows he's dying.

They've been fashioning his tombstone for weeks,
Deeply incised, his significant statue elegant,
Helmeted, barefoot, gripping his quiver and bow
While snow continues falling into the forest.
Terrific flashes of light are in his head

And everything is breaking up. He'll manage.
One of his names is Abdes, servant of Isis,

And she will put him back together again.
The Panther is sixty-two and will die well.
His last performance as an archer

Was killing a German on the ice,
The Rhine frozen from shore to shore.
Something wonderful happened. What was that?
Spelt. Marjoram. Onions. Sausages. Suffering light
And it all seemed like a good idea at the time.

AN OLD SOLDIER WHO SERVED
IN THE AMERICAN ARMY OF OCCUPATION
REVISITS BINGERBRÜCK,
AT THE CONFLUENCE
OF THE NAHE AND RHINE,
AND THINKS AGAIN
OF TIBERIUS JULIUS ABDES PANTERA

—for Thomas Kennedy

This steady rain and the Rhine in flood are commonplace,
The clouds draining down the mountains on both sides
For centuries, the brown to golden forest floor.
He lies on a pallet in the local sculptor's shop
To watch his tombstone being painted vividly,
The fine red cape, the green skirt, becoming vivid there.

Forty years of service, a common soldier, an archer,
Mention of his cult, mention he's Sidonian,
The Roman version of name, rank, and serial number.
His breath grows shallow and difficult as the end approaches.

Soon he'll be cremated according to the rules
And his body brightly colored will stand beside the road,
Right knee cocked gracefully. There are his long feet and toe
His sandals painted on, big, intelligent ears,
Hair cropped short in the usual honorable way,
O wonderful gaudy figure that must fade in time,
Finally to become a ghostly form of limestone.
Surely he's our one relic of the Holy Family
While the rain falls often as not on the Nahe and Rhine—
Ninety percent cloud cover, fifty percent of the time.

MARY
SHORTLY AFTER THE DEATH OF JOSEPH

When Joseph died, all of the children cried
Except for Jesus, who was healing the sick
And raising the dead well out of Nazareth.
James, who'd followed his half-brother, did come home
For the burial, saying Jesus was indisposed.
Joseph was in the ground within a day
According to our practices.

                       The grief
We felt for Joseph was commonplace and good.
We buried him deeper than the dogs could go.
Let the dead bury the dead.

                      Well, I wasn't dead
And neither were our sons and daughters there,
And here's another simple observation:

When all the dead are raised, at the last trump,
Joseph, I pray, will not be recreated
In any form he wouldn't understand.

When he awakens, may he be here in our old bed
In Galilee, up from oblivion,
Aware of my body and the smell of me,
I'm brave to say. But that's impossible.
It was terrible to realize he wasn't breathing.

GABRIEL VISITED ABDES PANTERA,
DISPLAYED HIMSELF AND SPOKE TO HIM,
BUT THERE WAS NO RESPONSE OF ANY KIND.
FIGURE WHY.

Wearing my specialty wings, the ruddy ones,
Cinquecento, I stooped through April rain
To just above the Rhine at Bingerbrück,
Shrugged, continued motioning gracefully

Toward the bowyer-archer on his shingle,
Who was done with practicing his shots
From shore to shore.
                    He didn't seem to see me,
But maybe he would listen

To the four languages I knew he knew—
Sidonian Aramaic, Levantine Greek,

And of course his soldier Latin,
And finally the local whitebread German tongue.

I was so fluttering because he's beautiful
In the sturdy way of soldier artisans—
He's a master of composite bows,
The seven woods, sinew, bone and glue.

O I was positive he'd love the news
And the flashing bearer of it: I 'M GABRIEL!
HAIL ABDES PANTERA! YOU THE MAN!
YOUR SON IN GALILEE IS MAGICAL.

PAUL OF TARSUS
TAKES SOME NOTES ABOUT THE GOSSIP
HE'LL NEVER MENTION IN A LETTER

Who cares if our Savior was a bastard?
His mother not a virgin? What if she groaned
Like all creation when she bore the Christ,
The issue of her passion for an archer,
A soldier, a creature of the corrupted world?
God in Christ will make of anything
A new creation. I hope he saved the Panther.
We're not afraid of pagans and the cults
Who have their virgin births and resurrections,
Old tents of flesh restitched. We rise on fire.
Better to have started at the bloody bottom,
God's son come from a Galilean hairdresser
And Eros out of Sidon with his arrows.
I love it! They say he worshipped Mother Isis.

God's natural father deserves our Victory.
Thank god my horse stumbled and fell on me
And bashed my skull into the light. The Light!
I never liked my mother more than Jesus
Loved the girl who saw him crucified.

MARY DREAMS HER ROLE

After the crucifixion and resurrection
I had a marvelous dream, and sometimes still do,
About how I'll represent another's love
And be a colorful queenly presence forever
As a fairly modest sensuous Jewish woman
From elsewhere in the Empire, including grief
Beneath the Cross, with Jesus in my arms.

From Galilee I've caused a world of trouble,
So I'm pleased to become a kindly image
But truth be told, possessive poet John
Never let me get close to the Cross
Or the pearly corpse the Panther and I created.

I never got to see our risen son
Though every other Mary seems to have
And numerous apostles, and pretty linen boys
Who'd come around to be initiated.

WATCHING MARY SLEEP,
SWEETLY AWKWARD GABRIEL
RECOUNTS THE CENTRAL PARADOX
OF THE ANNUNCIATION

I say to Mary, wake up, lovely, you're a virgin!
Those ladies and babies you've seen in dreams are you
And Jesus in the future, strange to say.
History has need of what you weren't
And will find hard your existential purity,
But please don't be afraid. You are afraid.

Fear not, for I'm your timeless friendly messenger.
I'm Gabriel, interpreter of dreams,
Saint of the telegraph and telephone–Benedict XV
Said so in 1921. She is stirring.
She's dreaming golden or peachy babies and ladies
In pictures and also statues pale. She sees
Temples, hears complicated glorious music

And is afraid, sees devils on the roofs,
Hears people praying to her at their deaths,
And she is dying, suffering the way all creatures do.

Mary, you are the Mother of God! You are
Wrung out by life and love, hope and desire,
The archer and the carpenter, the children.
That's how the best of virgins come to be!

MARY ON JOSEPH

Lord, I've been a problem all my life,
Especially after the Panther. Joseph lied
And said he got to me before the wedding
And was rebuked by numerous local elders.

Decent heavy Joseph at his lathe,
He got me sons and daughters with little romance,
Down-home loving when we wanted to,
And I made a strong point of patting him
And holding his hands on the streets of Nazareth.

Love comes in various sizes, and I loved his,
While Jesus was getting stranger, year after year,
Preparing to raise hell eternally.
I'm talking Joseph. He was good in bed.
My pretty archer always on the ground.

MARY THE MOTHER OF JESUS
IS WELL ON TOWARD THE END
AND TRIES TO TELL HERSELF
THE TRUTH ABOUT HER FEELINGS
FOR HER SON
AND WHY SHE FOLLOWS HIM

Simple James and Juda follow him,
Their outrageous half brother, and so of course do I,
In spite of how he always treated me.
Woman, what do I have to do with thee?
Fairly describes our bad relationship.
But O I wept to see him crucified.
My God, my God, why hast thou forsaken me?
He was always a magical needy boy.
Also he called down to John, *Behold thy mother!*
So from that time I've stayed with poet John.

Life's horrible or marvelous or dull,
And Jesus was serious trouble from day one on,
Conceived in me by a beautiful angel archer

Who practiced on the trunks of olive trees,
And shot our rats, and one time killed a bird
In merry flight. He also crippled a wolf.
The Panther, Lord, I wanted him in me,
And soon, behind a red boulder, he was,
Beneath a moon as round as my belly would be.
I follow our son who's risen from the dead.

WALKING WITH THE POET,
GABRIEL IS PLEASED BY THE DARK FOREST
WHERE ARMINIUS AND GERMANICUS FOUGHT
IN 16 AD NEAR IDISTAVISO,
THOUGH FOR A MOMENT
HE LOSES HEART

This is without question the dark forest
Magisterial! Cries Gabriel,
Loquacious, literary angel, best
Of company while figuring the past.
He's far from the deserts where he was imagined.
He's hovering just above the fallen leaves,
Two thousand years of oak and mountain ash,
That have maintained these longs walls of earth.
Gabriel, urbane, a dandy to tell the truth,
Now flying near the canopy, is pleased,
Saying, This dapple of greeny summertime
Moves me to wonder, *Am I necessary?*
These Germans with their metal arabesques,
And Romans with their roads and water courses,

In spite of the slaughter they made together,
Weren't less than our dusty sons of Abraham,
Except for one of *my* inventions.
He flutters down beside me here, whispers,
Mary, who is at least The Holy Ghost,
The way I imagine, is lovelier than trees,
More powerful than mountainsides.

AMIENS AND CHARTRES
AND THE LAST HAT I EVER WORE

I know as well as anyone the tricks
A famous place will try to play on us,
Our betters having written all those books
About octagonal spires or the cruise
Among the islands where our hearts must change.

Sometimes—Amiens—little happens—a church
We know has the highest ceiling does not derange
Our normal senses. We begin to think of lunch.
We try *not* to think of lunch, or of Chartres,
Where, walking the labyrinth, I cried
A little for nothing in particular.

One time a high wind blew off my hat
And as it rolled away, probably in Denver,
I was so pleased I teared up and smiled.

Even at this Extreme

TRAVELING WITH JIM

After Mont St. Michel and Chartres, we felt just a little let down by Amiens, magnificent as it was. "We should have come here first," Jim said, "we would have appreciated it more." But, great churches behind, we had come for the Somme—and it gave us more than we bargained for, almost more than we could stand.

A late May Sunday evening drive into the countryside and the first British graveyard, though carefully groomed as all of them were, was so inconspicuous that we almost passed it by. So we walked among the identical Portland stone monuments, reading the names—Pvt. William Miller, 1897-1916, "Oh, Shit."; Pvt. Henry Thompson, 1874-1916, "Forty-two! What the hell was he doing out here!"—and, on some, the inscriptions. We both shook our heads and softly groaned at the old lie "Dulce et Decorum Est," thinking of our own male children, but it was the very next grave that brought us simultaneously to one knee with gulping sobs: "Lord, give us the strength to bear our loss." "Goddamn," Jim said, "Goddamn!"

We spent the entire next day out there at, maybe, two dozen of those places, big and small, but we never got over that first one. As we walked through one of the largest, hard by the Aisne, it seemed, suddenly, as if every jet fighter in the French Air Force was shrieking overhead. Jim, the anti-pacifist, screamed back: "You're still at it, you bastards; you dumb bastards!" After that and much more, at long last, overwhelmed, I declared my heart-wearied inability to count another stone. "I'm glad you finally said something," he replied, "I'm sure enough ready to go." So, we stopped in a little village, where, long after lunch hours, the kind bistro owner, understanding, served us beer and special omelets. Somehow, not even Buchenwald got to us like the Somme.

Once on a Channel steamer going back to England, Whitehead, by chance, but not by accident, sat down next to a former mistress of Samuel Beckett and we had a long and lovely talk about life and art. That's always the way it was, traveling with Jim.

IN SEARCH OF THE PANTHER

I'm not exactly sure when Tiberius Julius Abdes Pantera, the Panther, came into Whitehead's life, but once he encountered that Sidonian archer almost nothing, except for Gen and the children, and perhaps the Razorback football or basketball team—depending on the season—so encompassed Jim's thought and work. Panther hunting drove him, lacking a word of German, to visit the *Römerhalle* in a small Rhenish town, where, with an earful of loud, slow, insistent Mississippi drawl, the staff woman, Englishless, turned in a panic to Fräulein Hornung, researching pre-history and wonderfully bi-lingual. That was the spark that set off the power train that led to Bad Kreuznach, with Mary and me along for the ride, where we established the link with bright, lovely Sabine Hornung and gentle, astute Peter Haupt, scholars, sweetly disposed. Jim fell in love with both "the German kids," as he always called them. He went back one more time and they conducted him on a tour of battlefields in the forest, near Idistaviso, where our Sidonian archer probably fought when the Romans wreaked terrible vengeance upon Germanic hordes for the loss of Quinctilius Varus's legions.

We drove out to Bingerbrück and stood in the mist on a hill overlooking the old train station and the Nahe where it flows into the Rhine, the clouds hanging low and grey over the wooded slopes on either side of the river. "Jesus," Jim declared, "a man from the sunny Sidon couldn't have cared much for this kind of dreary." "It's a typical German day," I replied, "like they always told us in the Army, 'ninety percent cloud cover, fifty percent of the time.'" "Damn," he grunted, "I hope the man liked his work."

Jim called to talk about the Panther on a hot August day just before Mary and I set off for Cape Breton by way of Cincinnati, the town with a properly Roman namesake. He was excited about having very nearly finished his Panther script and made me—there at the creation, as it were—promise to come over and read it as soon as we returned from Acadia. Six days later a few miles outside of Buffalo, our son called to tell us that James T. Whitehead had expired. So, Jim had carried the Panther until he couldn't carry any more.

Still not entirely believing, we turned back towards Fayetteville and all during that long, sad, quiet journey, I dug through my brain for a poem about friendship I had learned in college and never quite forgot:

They told me, Heraclitus, they told me you were dead,

They brought me bitter news to hear and bitter tears to shed.

I wept as I remember'd how often you and I

Had tired the sun with talking and sent him down the sky.

. . .

Still are thy pleasant voices, thy nightingales awake;

For Death, he taketh all away, but them he cannot take.

William Johnson Cory (1823-1892)

* * *

Jim's last lovely voices are what Michael Burns has gathered here. I miss Jim every day, but for all that Death has taken, he'll never take these away.

THE PANTHER AND THE JESUS DYNASTY

I think of Jim and James Tabor as pilgrims, coming from opposite directions, moving with uncertain steps in search of the same mysterious Grail. It is a sadness they did not stumble upon one another at some odd place along the road. There would have been loud talk, fierce argument and lots of laughter; it's a great pity, indeed, when such friends never have the opportunity to meet. But, then, they are, finally, meeting on these pages in the only way left to them. Jim would be happy for it, even at this extreme.

Tom Kennedy
January 2007

Biographies

James T. Whitehead (1936-2003)

In 1965, Whitehead and his friend, William Harrison, founded the nationally-prestigious Creative Writing Program at the University of Arkansas, Fayetteville. He taught in that program for the next thirty-four years, from 1965 to 1999. He was recipient of a Guggenheim Fellowship in fiction and a Robert Frost Fellowship in poetry. In 1981, Whitehead presented Jimmy Carter with a poem to honor his presidency and welcome him back to Plains, Georgia. Whitehead's sports novel, *Joiner* (1971), was listed among *The New York Times'* Noteworthy Books of the Year. While winning acclaim as a novelist, Whitehead published widely as a poet; his many, well-received collections include *Domains* (1967), *Local Men* (1979), the chapbook, *Actual Size* (1985), and *Near at Hand* (1993). With his untimely passing, Whitehead left a large body of work unpublished: two novel manuscripts, several screen plays, and scores of poems. It is from out of these posthumous materials that the current collection has been gathered.

James D. Tabor

Author of *Things Unutterable: Paul's Ascent to Paradise* (1984) and *The Jesus Dynasty: The Hidden History of Jesus, His Royal Family, and the Birth of Christianity* (2006), Tabor is Head of the Department of Religious Studies at University of North Carolina, Charlotte, where he has taught since 1989. A renowned Biblical scholar, Tabor has appeared in documentaries and lectured worldwide on the Dead Sea Scrolls, the Scriptural accounts of Jesus's birth, the purported Jesus ossuary, and the Scriptural-archaeological evidence surrounding Pantera.

Michael D. Burns

Author of *When All Else Failed* (1984), *The Secret Names* (1994), and *It Will Be All Right in the Morning* (1998), Burns is Professor of English at Missouri State University, where he has taught creative writing since 1987. Recipient of The Porter Prize and an NEA Fellowship for poetry, Burns was a student of Whitehead's in the Creative Writing Program at the University of Arkansas. In addition to *The Panther,* Burn has co-edited (with Jessica Glover) *Common Need: New and Selected Poems by James T. Whitehead,* forthcoming from the University of Evansville Press.